Quitterie and Daniel Cazes

Discovering
Toulouse

**Photographs by Bertrand Cabrol, by Pascal Moulin
and Guy-Marie Renié**

Translated by Peter Hackett and Angela Moyon

ÉDITIONS SUD OUEST

The Pont-Neuf (16th – 17th C) and the Église de la Dalbade.

Toulouse has always been the gateway to the Midi: regularly swept by the south winds, the city offers visitors access to a Mediterranean world thanks to its geographical location, its climate, and its culture. Today, the personality of this large metropolis, often divided between tradition and modernity, is the result of its history and the men who shaped it. Beyond the vision of a "pink city" which emerges from a superficial regard, Toulouse was "Palladian" that is to say receptive to the arts, "holy" for its dozens of churches, and commercial and agricultural because it always knew how to profit from its situation and its environment. The city's building materials take the visitor back to Antiquity: brick has been the dominant building material in Toulouse for more than twenty centuries. The prices of stone which had to be transported by boat were well-known: marble from the Pyrenees and limestone brought by way of the Garonne River, overshadowed since the 17th century by marble from Caunes-Minervois in the Aude region and stone brought from Carcassonne by way of the Canal du Midi.

Little remains of the glorious Antiquity of Toulouse. Here and there, vestiges of the rampart surrounding the city at the beginning of the first century A.D. can be seen. This enclosure, useful only for prestige in these times of peace, once symbolised the city's might. Toulouse owed its fortune to the fact that it was a meeting point for trade between the Mediterranean Sea and the Atlantic, more than any other port on the Garonne, onto which the city freely opened. It was only in the third century that the insecurity of the times prompted the construction of a new rampart along the river (visible at the Institut Catholique). The Roman monuments have disappeared: although the remains of one of the largest theaters in the Roman world, have been found near the Pont-Neuf and althouh the aqueduct still appeared on maps of the city in the 17th century, the forum temple podium (probably the Capitole), was identified and partly destroyed in 1992, in Place Esquirol; the other temples, public buildings and houses only exist as scattered traces. Antiquity survives nonetheless in the orthogonal layout of the city's central streets, parting from the principal north-south artery, which is now a pedestrian zone (Rue Saint-Rome, Rue des Changes, Rue des Filatiers). The end of Antiquity brought the churches: in the center, the cathedral and the Daurade…; outside the walls the funereal basilicas, the most noteworthy of which is Saint-Sernin. We know little of the "congested capital" (described by Mr. Roquebert) of the Visigoth kingdom (between 418 and 507) nor of the famous « Reino

de Tolosa » that the Spanish consider as the foundation of their own monarchy. The following centuries remain quite obscure. Urban development began after the year 1000. The city's expansion towards the North, begun in the 11th century, is demarcated by another rampart. Saint Sernin was the center of the new Bourg, accompanied by Saint-Pierre-des-Cuisines on the bank of the Garonne. Another district, Saint-Cyprien, sprang up on the opposite bank and was also surrounded by a rampart in the 14th century.

From the end of the 11th century to the 14th century, religious architecture saw a period of effervescence and renewal; the same was certainly true for secular architecture, about which less is known. Toulouse came under the dominion of the king of France in 1271, after three centuries during which at its apogee, it dominated the Midi as far East as the Rhône. After the disastrous period of the wars, the famines and the plagues of the 14th century, the city recovered its vitality with the revival of trade and experienced a true golden age beginning in the middle of the 15th century with the growth in pastel farming. Dazzling fortunes were built and resulted in the creation of mansions, which were often veritable palaces. Wealth opened the doors of the noblesse de robe to certain members of the bourgeoisie, whether by carefully arranged marriages

or by accession to the ennobling post of magistrate. The collapse in the pastel trade and the wars of Religion caused a new era of difficulties. However, thanks to the traditional farming of wheat, which could be marketed by way of the Canal du Midi – that extraordinary economic tool – the bourgeois were able to safely establish their fortunes. The city was then able to install facilities, which, apart from pleasure and prestige, also served the needs of trade (promenades around the Grand-Rond, construction of the façade of the Hôtel de Ville and the Place du Capitole, renovation of the wharves…). In the 19th century, these revenues were no longer sufficient, and industry failed to develop. Caught up in the fever of grand city planning inspired by Baron Haussman, Toulouse installed two large avenues – Rue d'Alsace-Lorraine and Rue de Metz – whose buildings clearly demonstrate the break, which they represent with traditional values.

Now in full expansion, invigorated by prestigious industries, Toulouse is searching for its identity and sometimes finding it. Endowed with an image of vitality, the city continues to expand its facilities - by sometimes denying the richness of its past – and rediscovers its brick façades and its former aspects, but still hesitates. Pastiche dominates local architecture, the city's culture only timidly dares

The model of the Temple du Capitole
(1st century A.D.)
in the Musée Saint-Raymond.

At the center of the Place Wilson,
the garden with the statue
of the native Languedoc poet Goudouli (1580-1649).

to embrace the contemporary. But the vibrant charm of its narrow streets, the moving beauty of certain spots, the pleasure of losing oneself in other times, invite the visitor to stroll, to become a resident of the city; this is the discovery to which we invite you.

The Place Wilson

Since its creation in the 19th century under the name of the Place Villeneuve, the Place Wilson is the monumental entrance to the heart of Toulouse. The plan to renovate this space, formed by the meeting of the antique Rempart de la Cité and the medieval Rempart du Bourg, took form between 1805 and 1834. A large avenue (the present day Allées Jean-Jaurès) leading from the Canal du Midi to the oval square opened a large breach in the belt formed by the boulevards. Today, these radiating streets provide access to several neighborhoods of the city. The fountain, the statue of Goudouli and the vegetation represent the mildness of life and temper the rigid order of the brick buildings, far-removed heirs of the "insulae" of Rome and Ostia.

OPPOSITE PAGE

The Capitole façade:
a superb 18th century Hôtel de Ville with a prestigious name.

The Capitole

The term Capitole evokes more an antique temple than a city hall, and yet there was indeed a Capitole in Toulouse, a Roman sanctuary dedicated to Jupiter, Juno and Minerva. It was in fact, a very large temple with a façade, measuring 27 meters (one of the two most largest discovered in France together with the Narbonne Capitole) identified in 1992 during the archeological dig in the Place Esquirol. The results of these finds allowed a model to be constructed (which is in the Musée Saint-Raymond) which repositions the building in the vast forum square whose double colonnaded porticos led on to numerous public buildings. The memory of the former Roman municipal council magistrates' meetings in this building were perpetuated and, in the Middle Ages, the people of Toulouse, taking advantage of the similarity between the words capitum (chapter) and capitolium (Capitole), took this prestigious name for their Hôtel de Ville or City Hall.

In the 12th century, the representatives of the new commercial class took the distinguished title of "consul" (later changing it to "capitoul"), and together with the judges nominated by the count, arbitrated affairs between merchants in the Maison Commune. At the end of the 12th century, they possessed numerous regulatory, judicial and military powers. After 1271, the kings of France confirmed their privileges, but their powers were gradually taken over, first by the seneschal, then by the Parliament

AT LEFT

Salle des Illustres in the Capitole,
created between 1892 and 1898 by Paul Pujol,
it is decorated with paintings and sculptures
by Jean-Paul Laurens, Benjamin Constant, Rixens...

View of the Cour Henri IV with, in the background,
the portal designed by Nicolas Bachelier (16th century).

The "donjon du Capitole",
erected at the beginning
of the 16th century,
and crowned with
a belfry in 1873
by Eugène Viollet-le-Duc.

beginning in 1443, and finally, by the Intendant of the Languedoc, beginning in the 17th century.

The acquisition of buildings by the consuls in 1190 represented their desire to establish themselves as a distinct power, at the opposite end of the City from the residence of the count. The magistrates, who remained in office for a term of only a year, never succeeded in constructing a coherent monumental group of buildings.

In the small district which gradually took form on the current site of the Capitole and the Square Charles de Gaulle, a number of large buildings were constructed in the Middle Ages and coldly demolished in the 19th century. The one remaining is the "Donjon", the former Tour des Archives completed in 1530; its slate roof was redone in 1873 by Viollet-le-Duc, who also added a belfry. Currently a passage between the Place and the Square, the Cour Henri IV was built at the very beginning of the 17th century according to the plans of the architect Souffron; the portal, built by Bachelier in 1546, is topped by a statue of the king. The current façade, designed by Guillaume Cammas, was intended to conceal the heterogeneous buildings of the old Maison Commune. Construction began in 1750, when the square did not yet exist (it would not be finished until a century later). From the classical rhythm of Cammas' elevation,

emerges the central portico; the eight columns in marble from the Caunes region symbolizing the eight magistrates, support a pediment decorated with statues of Force and Justice. The north portico is crowned with statues of Clemence Isaure and Pallas, and the southern portico bears the images of Tragedy and Comedy. The imposing façade was replicated on the side facing the square in 1883-84.

After Bachelier's, a large stairway provides access to ceremonial rooms: the Salle Henri-Martin, the Salle du Conseil Municipal, the Galerie des Illustres. Paintings from the end of the 19th and the beginning of the 20th centuries glorify grand events in the city's history.

Henri Martin created an exceptional set of paintings: some panels represent the Seasons, others show the banks of the Garonne (where Jean Jaurès can be seen in an off-white overcoat). The great Galerie des Illustres, renovated at the end of the 19th century, has received paintings, busts and stucco works from the greatest of Toulouse's artists. Recent restoration work has brought back all its former brillance.

The Capitole is also the theatre of the same name, which is located in the southern wing of the city hall. In recent years, restoration work together with considerable technical restructuring has been undertaken to comply with the

The Rue du Taur

The Rue du Taur leads from the Place du Capitole, which was laid out in the 18th and 19th centuries, on the site of the large northern gate of the Roman city (the last remains of which were demolished in 1971), to the Basilique Saint-Sernin. With its adjacent streets, where can be seen old schools and the municipal library (one of largest in France), with its shops selling new and second-hand books, it continues the Bourg's University tradition, dating from the Middle Ages. The presence of the Tour Maurand (a vestige of a 12th century fortified manor), of 17th and 18th century houses and the proximity of convents provide an introduction to the city's complexity. Today this street is the major tourist thoroughfare of Toulouse, uniting the old southern districts to that exemplary pair of buildings: the Église Saint-Sernin and the Musée Saint-Raymond. At number 69, the Renaissance doorway of the former Collège de l'Esquile is not to be missed (constructed in 1555 by Nicolas Bachelier). Crossing the threshold, one enters a large courtyard bordered on the left by the recently revealed traces of a medieval house. Two windows and a fireplace are now quite visible. Five classical arcades form the backdrop to this courtyard, giving access to the new Toulouse Film Archive, the second in France and one of the largest in Europe, inaugurated in 1997. The large courtyard with its levels of arcatures (rows of small arcades) superimposed on the Collège de l'Esquile building, is worth a detour. Access is by the imposing doorway of N°1 of the street of the same name.

At N° 56 Rue du Taur, set in a huge courtyard, punctuated by the arcades of the former Grand Seminaire buildings, the remains still exist of a wooden medieval gallery which led to the Collège du Perigord buildings.

The Église du Taur

With its mighty façade topped by the cowled arches of the steeple, the Église du Taur fits in the alignment of the houses on the street, a disposition which has become relatively rare. The name recalls the legend of Saturnin's body being dragged by a bull (see Saint-Sernin). Mentioned in the 12th century as a possession of Saint-Sernin, the church was rebuilt around 1300; its single nave had three bays. In the 14th century, two larger bays were added onto the eastern section and amplified by lateral chapels and the choir. The whole was arranged in an original manner: between two chapels was built another, that for some time held the shroud of Cadouin (which has since been returned to the abbey, in the Perigord). The shroud, which is said to come from Antioch, was transported to Toulouse during the Hundred Years War, and it is claimed that it worked a number of miracles. It was authenticated in 1935 as being of Moslem origin and dating from the early 12th century. The church's current

Few Toulouse residents
know of the Collège de Foix.
Nonetheless, it is one of the rare
15th century buildings
still standing in Toulouse,
and it is a charming representation
of the architecture of mediaeval
university student colleges.
The narrow brickwindows
illuminate its famous library.

dusty décor is somewhat sad. Nonetheless, on the south wall of the third bay of the nave, there remain traces of a 14th century painting, showing thirty-eight persons representing the genealogy of Jacob. Murals by Bernard Bénézet and a large canvas by Jean-Louis Bézard, all dating from the 19th century, illustrate the martyrdom of Saturnin.

The Collège de Foix

Forgotten today in the charms of a secret garden, the Collège de Foix is the creation of a patron cardinal, Pierre de Foix, papal legate of Avignon. This religious foundation was to provide free housing for 25 poor and deserving students of civil law, canon law and theology. It was constructed by the head builder Jean Constantin between 1457 and 1460. The four fine brick-built gothic galleries of the courtyard (visible from N°2 Rue Deville) provided access to various rooms, offices, dormitories, and bedrooms necessary for student life. To the West, was built the chapel (demolished in the 19th century). The main building still dominates the college, with its mirandes (doubtless added later), its angled turrets and its open windows in austere brick walls. A vast vaulted room, with intersecting ribs, on the ground floor, held a precious library of manuscripts which were acquired by the cardinal after the death

of the anti-pope Benoît XIII, sold to Colbert in the 17th century, and which are now stored in the Bibliothèque Nationale. Nowadays chapel for the community of the Nuns of Compassion who occupy the former college, it is accessible only during the times of religious services. Access is from N°11 Rue des Lois.

Two notable changes affected city life in the 13th century: the appearance of the mendicant orders and the creation of the University (1229). With the latter, a new type of structure was instituted; the colleges, or student hostels. These were designed to house poor students and provide them with spiritual as well as material security. In 1243, a rich bourgeois, Vidal Gautier, founded the first one for 20 poor students. Until the beginning of the 14th century, the other hostels were created by the great monastic orders, in order that monks (from Grandselve, from Moissac…) could study in Toulouse.

Then, in 1319, the Collège de Montlauzun, and in 1337, the Collège de Verdale introduced a more efficient formula: the college was to be a charitable foundation, for the eternal rest of the donor's soul, specifically oriented towards the University (the students had to know how to read and to show a capacity for learning) and with a spiritual goal (numerous religious rites were scheduled).

The Couvent des Cordeliers

The Cordeliers (a minor order of Franciscan friars) moved to Toulouse in 1222. Nothing remains of the early buildings and little of the large monastery built from the 13th to the 15th century. The church (13th to 14th century), of which remains the steeple, a piece of the wall of the apse and the portal, was built on a large scale: 86 meters long, 27 meters wide and 26 meters high. With a single nave, it had the same outer appearance as the Église des Jacobins: a pentagonal apse with tall choir stalls, in prolongation of the nave, high buttresses linked by transverse arcs, chapels lodged betweens the buttresses. After being allotted in 1818 to the military, which used it as a fodder storehouse, it burned down in 1871. Rather than restore it, the church was demolished, thus causing the loss to Toulouse of one of its most important building of the Middle Ages. It was complemented by a large chapel, on the southwest side, built by Jean Tissendier, the bishop of Rieux, between 1322 and 1347. It was demolished in the first half of the 19th century. Statues of the apostles, of Franciscan saints, of Christ and the Virgin Mary, of Jean Tissandier, as the donor, as well as the recumbent statue from the bishop's tomb were taken from it and are preserved at the Musée des Augustins (except for two at the Musée Bonnat in Bayonne). The visitor can still admire the chapter house, with its vaulted ceiling which rests on two slender cylindrical columns. Entrance to the "Forum des Cordeliers" is by N° 15 Rue des Lois. The courtyard of N° 13 in this same street leads to the finely vaulted 14th century sacristy (private property) recently restored.

The Chapelle des Carmélites

Built from the beginning of 1622, the chapel is the only remaining vestige of the Couvent des Carmélites, which reached almost to the site of the municipal library, in the Rue de Périgord. Its architecture is simple, a single nave with four bays completed by a three-sided apse. Its vault is built of oak panelling with supporting ribs. At the end of the 17th century, Jean-Pierre Rivalz decorated the high parts between the windows with paintings of the Seven Virtus inspired by the Chapelle Sistine. The decoration was completed in the middle of the following century by Jean-Baptiste Despax, who produced here what is considered as the masterpiece of the city's painting from that era. Three subjects of Carmélites meditation were illustrated: the incarnation of Christ with a part devoted to childhood, the wonders realized by the prophet Elijah and his disciple Elisha, the founders of the religious community on Mount Carmel and the glorification of Saint Theresa of Avila, the reformer of Carmel, canonized the year of the founding of the chapel.

The portal and steeple of the Église des Cordeliers, the remains of one of the largest Gothic convents constructed in Toulouse in the 13th and 14th centuries.

AT RIGHT
Saint-Sernin from the south; the upper parts of the building have been recently restored to their former aspect, before the 19th century restoration work conducted by E. Viollet-le-Duc.

The Basilique Saint-Sernin

The story of the first bishop of Toulouse is already known from the account of his Passion written in the 5th century. This account relates how Saturnin (transformed into Sernin in Occitan) was martyred in 250 A.D; while he was on the way to his church, he was recognized by pagans who blamed him for the failure of the sacrifices they offered to their gods. They tied him to a bull which tumbled down the steps of the Temple du Capitole, left the City by its northen gate and disappeared into the countryside. The body of Saturnin was buried by two women, the "Saintes Puelles" in the necropolis which lay on either side of Cahors roadway. Hilaire, his successor in the fourth century, built a small wooden church above his tomb. Due to the large

The Basilique Saint-Sernin viewed from the north; until the beginning of the 19th century, a massive cloister and canonical buildings were erected against the north flank of the nave.

The Porte des Comtes owes its name to the nearby funereal niche housing the tombs of the Counts of Toulouse, in their early Christian sarcophagi which doubtless originated in the necropolis around the first basilica.

OPPOSITE PAGE
The principal nave, the galleries and the sanctuary of the Basilique Saint-Sernin.

number of worshippers, and because the burial sites had multiplied around the holy grave, Bishop Exupère built a large basilica, to which the remains of the saint were transferred in 402 or 403. A monastery, mentioned in 844, was built to guard the tomb.

In the middle of the 11th century, this first church no longer met the needs of the many pilgrims who came to pray near the numerous relics stored in the sanctuary. In the third quarter of the 11th century, construction began on the chevet of the vast church which we know today, with its monumental transept, each wing of which includes two facing apses, and the choir surrounded by an ambulatory, providing access to five radiating chapels. Outside, the terracing of the structure from the radiating chapels to the emergence of the steeple, offers the eye a balanced progression, and the color contrast provided by the joint use of brick and stone gives life to this mighty structure. Inside, galleries are situated above the aisles of the transept and those of the choir bay, their vaults buttressing those of the upper portion of the chevet. At the intersection of the transept, covered by a cupola, supported by squinches, rises the steeple. At the very deepest part of this vast edifice, in the crypt, was kept the tomb of Saturnin, visited by the pilgrims.

Sculpture played a major role from the beginning of the basilica's construction, with close to 260 capitals on the inside and portals on the outside decorated with narrative scenes. The Porte des Comtes, constructed beginning in 1082-83, was monumentally decorated. Under the decorated cornices are three mutilated relief sculptures (the center relief depicted Saint Saturnin between two lions), sitting above the double passage. In the passage, the capitals evoke the parables of the wicked rich man and of Lazarus, representations of the theme of Salvation and Damnation.

In the next funerary niche are placed several sarcophagi from the first Christian era, re-used as tombs for the Counts of Toulouse and their family members. The middle one has been replaced by a mould; the original, whose lateral sculptures (portrait of Saint-Sepulcre in medaillon) are very rare, is placed in the western side aisle of the north transom of the transept.

In 1096, the work had progressed sufficiently to allow the installation of the table of the main altar. Sculpted by Bernard Gilduin, in turn inspired by ancient examples. Pope Urban II himself consecrated the church and the altar.

In 1118, probable date of the death of canon Raymond Gayrard, to whom the overseeing of the construction is

The inscription which runs along the upper part of the altar recalls that "the fraternity of the holy martyred Saturnin established this altar on which the divine rite shall be celebrated for the salvation of their souls and that of all God's faithful". It was signed by the sculptor Bernard Gilduin. The different sides of the table are adorned by relief sculptures; a bust of Christ carried by angels looking away appears on the forward side, on the left he is surrounded by the Virgin and the apostles; other apostles are represented on the opposite side and the back is decorated with a frieze of birds facing one another.

Saint-Sernin: the tympanum over the Miègeville door, representing the Ascension of Christ, a masterpiece of Romanesque sculpture.

Detail of Romanesque paintings in the northern portion of the transept, showing the Angel of Resurrection and the Holy Women at the Tomb.

The chevet of the Basilique Saint-Sernin, an exceptional and monumental composition which directs the eye upwards towards the most singular example of a Middle Ages Toulouse steeple.

often attributed, the chevet was finished. The nave had reached the level of the high windows and was finished only in its three or four eastern bays. The nave continued the monumental portion of the transept, but with double aisles –a rarity during the Romanesque period. At the southern end, the Miègeville door received its decorations around 1115-1120. Carved figures support the upper cornice, the façade is decorated with the images of Saint Peter and Saint James the Greater. The tympanum, the essential and new element of the portal, develops the theme of the Ascension. Slightly further back, the western portal should have surpassed it in splendor, but the two doors without tympanum were surmounted with relief sculptures in marble which disappeared during the Revolution, with the exception of several quite remarkable sculptures which can be seen at the Musée des Augustins. Painted decorations covered the inside of the church beginning in the Romanesque period; the recent removal of whitewash, put on in the 19th century, revealed fragments of old paintings. The most complete composition is found in the northern portion of the transept: on the wall, the Resurrection of Christ takes five panels, and the Glory of the Lamb of God is

This capital, over the Miègeville portal, depicting the Annunciation and the Visitation, illustrates the theme of Redemption through Christ's coming.

depicted on the vault. The construction of the church continued during the Gothic era: at the same time that the tomb of Saint Saturnin was being raised under a canopy and the crypts were built (they were enlarged in the 17th century), the construction of the nave also continued towards the west. The original plans were respected, as well as the concept of the vault, giving the church its interior unity. Work began again on the roofing of the entire building. The steeple was raised in the second half of the 18th century. To ensure its stability, the supports of the transept crossing were reinforced. The Renaissance saw the work continuing on Saint-Sernin; new doors enlarged the entry to the crypts and new paintings covered the pillars of the transept, the walls and the vaults of the choir. 17th century builders wanted to provide more splendor for the presentation of the relics which were the reputation of the church. The relics, which had been kept in the ambulatory and its chapels, were placed in sculpted wood cabinets adorned with paintings and gilding, flanked with relief sculptures of great historical figures and surmounted by a pediment. This "Tour of Holy Bodies", removed by Viollet-le Duc in the name of unity of style, has been returned to its place in the

1970's thanks to the praiseworthy efforts of the Inspector General of Historic Buildings Georges Costa. With the work of the great architect and renovator Viollet-le-Duc, the 19th century was to leave a strong imprint on the building. His alterations to the interior have been erased for the most part by a recent and welcome restoration carried out by the Chief Architects for Historical Monuments, Sylvain Stym-Popper and Yves Boiret. On the exterior, Viollet-le-Duc modified the roof structure, so that the interior structure would be visible from the outside. He eliminated the tile coverings of the apses and replaced them with stone slabs. He also added ornaments...This work undertaken during the second half of the 19th century eventually posed certain problems regarding the preservation of the monument. Consequently, the building was returned to its approximate state before the works began.

The mediaeval Treasury of the Basilique Saint-Sernin, one of the most important among western churches, was unfortunately impoverished in the 16th century by the removal of an impressive and ancient cameo (the "gemma augustea"), which is nowadays in Vienna (Austria). At the Revolution, pieces of inestimable value were also removed

The Saint-Sernin crypt; keystone of the gothic canopy decorated with the Crowning of the Virgin (13th century).

as was in the 19th century the celebrated Book of Gospels of Charlemagne (now held in the Bibliothèque nationale de France). However, significant works of art have been retained. If the "Saint Exupère shroud" that extremely rare piece of 12th century material fabricated in Islamic Andalusia, cannot be systematically exposed to the light because of its extremely fragile nature, at least, the crypt displays in an enveloping atmosphere of mystery and warmth, several examples of the goldsmith's art, among which the extremely fine enamelled reliquary of the True Cross is especially noticeable (end of 12th century).

The Église Saint-Sernin (promoted to the rank of a basilica in 1878) was, until the Revolution, closely linked to the abbey buildings which surrounded it. If nothing is known of the earliest installations, the Romanesque era left prestigious structures, which were erased by the vandalism of the early 19th century. Among these were the great Romanesque cloister (several of its magnificent capitals are preserved at the Musée des Augustins), the chapter house, the abbot's dwelling and the canonical buildings. Today, in the middle of an oval square, the church emerges from an ocean of parked cars, slightly protected from their invasion by the fence of a small garden. The subtle combi-

nation of a detailed archaeological dig together with the new improvements to the square, should accentuate the historical aspect of this exceptional site and render it more accessible and more pleasant to the hundreds of thousands of tourists visiting it each year.

The Musée Saint-Raymond: Musée des Antiques de Toulouse

This building houses one of the principal collections of antiquities in France. The recent renovations have led to the discovery of an archaeological entity of major interest in the basement; the traces of a section of the early Christian necropolis which had developed around the tomb of Saturnin and the remains of a rare lime kiln into which a number of marble sarcophagi from this ancient cemetery had disappeared. A fine series of sarcophagi of this type, typical of the South-West France, almost all of them originating from the Saint-Sernin necropolis, is exhibited here in this place so full of atmosphere. Visiting this exhibition will complete your tour of the nearby Romanesque basilica. Here one can interpret the first Christian images of Toulouse and one can admire the sumptuous verdant decorations worked in vine, acanthus and ivy leaves. The walls of the

The Musée Saint-Raymond (view of the first floor) is situated in a former student hostel constructed in 1523 by Louis Privat.

original Hôpital Saint-Raymond (11th century), still exist here as well as those of the student hostel (13th century) of the same name, all of which were entirely rebuilt by Louis Privat, master mason, in 1523. It is this last classified historic building which has housed the museum since 1891.

On the second floor, ancient Tolosa comes to life. The old quarters in the center of Toulouse are still built upon the remains of Tolosa and the amphora, wine sets, inscriptions in Iberian and remarkable gold jewellery of the Volques Tectosages tell the story of the origins of this ancient town. Toulouse was conquered by the Romans in 106 B.C. and exhibited here is one of the oldest latin inscriptions in France, dated 47 B.C. The buildings and monuments constructed during the Roman Empire, have left eloquent traces of their former splendour here in this part of the museum. The Roman province of Narbonne, of which Toulouse was one of the principal towns, has provided the museum with significant works like the remarkable Julio-Claudian portrait groups, from Béziers and the Discobolus of Carcassonne. Some very fine bronzes have also been provided, among which the exceptionally sculpted chariot ornament, representing a panther attacking a rider, is particularly outstanding.

On the first floor is housed the largest collection of Greco-Roman sculptures so far discovered on French soil taken from the ruins of the Villa de Chiragan in Martres-Tolosane (Haute-Garonne). The first series is dedicated to the architecture of this genuine marble clad palace which developed into a building containing hundreds of rooms, porticos, courtyards and gardens spread over an area of thirteen hectares. The following series of sculpted panels showing the Labours of Hercules indicate the "Baroque" and Pergamon style of a great sculptor active during the 3rd century A.D. Chiragan was also, during the Empire, a true museum where replicas of works of art, of the finest quality from among the best known classic Greek sculptures, were assembled for exhibition. Myron's Athena, the Venus of Cnide and Praxiteles' Eros of Centocelle, the originals of which have long since disappeared, can still be admired by means of these copies in the Musée Saint-Raymond, together with a profusion of mythological sculptures in black marble (Pluto-Sarapis, Harpocrates, Isis) and the Abduction of Proserpine, the Bacchus etc..). The Emperor's Gallery constitutes the end of this spectacular tour, with the larger part of the sculpted portraits discovered during the dig at Chiragan. Here,

one can appreciate the whole range of the development of Roman portrait art from the end of the 1st century B.C. to the 5th century A.D.

On the ground floor, the Grand Tinel (16th century) holds temporary exhibitions, largely provided for by the treasures hidden in the museum storerooms (protohistoric art, Greek, Cypriot Roman art, upper Middle Ages art: coin collections and epigraphy). The Musée Saint-Raymond is responsible for not only public access to the main archaeological sites in the town (the crypt of Saint-Pierre-des-Cuisines, the Roman amphitheatre, the Ancely Baths), but also the conservation and caretaking of the Basilique Saint-Sernin in collaboration with the parish priest. Times of access and conditions concerning these various sites, which vary to a certain degree, can be ascertained by application to the museum.

Saint-Pierre-des-Cuisines

The story of the church began in the fourth and the fifth centuries, with the establishment of a necropolis and then a funereal basilica outside the walls of the antique City, the remains of which can be seen in the archaeological site in the crypt. This large building (almost 30 meters long) constructed from salvage materials, was modified during the upper Middle Ages by the installation of sarcophagi in the funereal niches carved in the thickness of the walls.

In the 11th century, the church and its attached grounds were given by the count of Toulouse to the abbey of Moissac, which established a priory on the site. Saint-Pierre-des-Cuisines then experienced a period of architectural development whose scale has recently been revealed by archaeological excavations. A larger choir, better adapted to the needs of the monks, was built and has recently been largely reconstructed. Those which however is quite genuine are the triumphal arch (where the choir opened into the nave), and a window where alternate brick and stone courses characterize the construction style of the end of the 11th century together with the western wall of the square steeple above the choir. The nave was later enlarged to include the previous building.

ABOVE

In front of the lofty brick architecture of the Église de Saint-Pierre-des-Cuisines, there exists a pretty tomb set in a Romanesque portal built into an opening: a marble sarcophagus placed on little columns is installed behind a clerestory. This funereal niche was once placed above the entrance gate of the parish cemeter,y which extended towards the east and the south of the church.

To the west, a powerful structure rose higher than the nave; its elevation can be seen from the outside in the left half of the façade: between two buttresses there is a wall, thicker towards the base, pierced by two arched windows; in the interior, the traces of the removal of a groined vault which once covered the lower level, can be seen.

In the 1180's a chevet chapel, roofed with one of the first ribbed vaults erected in Toulouse doubled the size of the Romanesque choir. Then, in the western extension, a side aisle attached to the Romanesque nave was constructed, composed of five spans. In the second of these spans a new portal was placed re-using the Romanesque capitals which had formerly belonged to the 12th century entrance. These capitals depict two narratives, one devoted to the life of Christ, the other to Saint Peter. Still in the south side, a mediaeval tomb, set inside a wall which once marked the border of the cemetery, shelters a sarcophagus; the arch in the middle of the recess is closed by an arcature supported by four columns. It was at the same period that the Romanesque nave was raised and vaulted as the two great ribbed arches, which are visible in the interior on the north side, indicate.

In the 14th century, the church saw the beginning of the completion of a major project which had as its aim the construction of a huge single nave, with a single-span vault 20 meters wide. The south wall of the Romanesque nave was knocked down and large high narrow windows pierced the south side, above the raised 13th century side aisle, (their upper portion shows that the planned height was never achieved) but the vaulting was never completed.

In the 16th century, the priory came under the control of the Carthusian order. At the time of the Revolution, the parish was transferred to Saint-Pierre-des-Chartreux and Saint-Pierre-des-Cuisines was transformed into a cannon

Saint-Pierre-des-Chartreux; Altar angels sculpted by François Lucas (18th century).

foundry before becoming a warehouse within the arsenal of the Army of the Pyrenees.

Nowadays transformed into an auditorium for the regional national Conservatoire, the former Église de Saint-Pierre-des-Cuisines has been converted and can be visited (information from the Musée Saint-Raymond).

Saint-Pierre-des-Chartreux

The Carthusian monks of Saïx, near Castres, took refuge in the Bourg of Toulouse in 1569 after being chased from their monastery by Protestants. They began to build their monastery in 1602. The architecture of the church clearly demonstrated its basic function: a dome marked the site of the altar, towards the street the three-bayed nave received the faithful and at the other end a large chorus of six bays was reserved for the monks. For two centuries, the greatest artists of Toulouse succeeded one another in the church, creating one of the city's most beautiful collections of classical art.

The church was dedicated to the Virgin Mary and Saint Paul the Hermit in 1612. A first dome had just been finished, with a wooden ceiling, and Pierre Monge had

sculpted the stalls of the monks. The decorations of the chorus grew richer, and in 1654 it was adorned with a series of paintings of scenes from the Gospel. In 1682, François Fayet painted a ten-panel work titled "Les Pères du Désert", alternating with panels showing the life of Saint Bruno.

Before 1752, Pierre Lucas completed the set with relief sculptures representing monastic, moral and theological virtues. In the 18th century, the first church was remodelled; it was heightened (the old walled-in windows can be clearly seen) and the dome, surmounted by the statue of Saint John the Baptist was redone. François Gammas provided the artwork on the plastered vault of the dome, where the Spirit of Antiquity manifested itself in the grand arches, the pilasters and the Corinthian capitals. He painted the monochrome designs on the arms of the transept and thought up the design of the altar. On the pedestal, François Lucas sculpted two angels in marble, set on either side of an ancient urn topped with a crucifix. The great delicacy of the angels' gestures, the disorder of the garments, the quality of the faces and the studied position of the bodies in order to avoid rigid symmetry , all make these angels, very Romanesque in spirit, a group full of dynamism and grace, "surprising in the chapel of an order known for the rigor of its mortifications." (Jean Rocacher).

But the riches of the church do not end there. There is also the wooden pulpit carved in the shape of the prow of a ship, the re-used Romanesque grilles and the sumptuous grilles of the 17th and 18th centuries which allow the different aspects of the art of Toulouse wrought ironwork to be appreciated.

The organs were provided by the Jacobins; the instrument was brought to the Église des Chartreux when it was dedicated to Saint Pierre and became the seat of the parish.

The Rempart du Bourg

These important remains of the medieval Rempart du Bourg have been conserved – or perhaps forgotten (?) – along a stretch 650 meters long. Four mighty towers still stretch along the straight rampart built in the 14th century and redone in the 16th century (nothing is known of the first rampart, dating from the 12th century). Numerous gates marked the points where city streets led out onto the neighbouring countryside; Porte du Bazacle, Las Crosses, Arnaud-Bernard, Pouzonville, Matabiau, Sardane, Villeneuve. Their memory remains in the names of nearby streets. On the filled-in trenches and the wooden palisades of the City and the Bourg, were established the boulevards which form the first city's inner beltway. On the opposite bank of the Garonne, the Quartier Saint-Cyprien was also protected by a surrounding wall in the 16th century; this wall, still visible from the Centre d'art moderne et contemporain called the Abattoirs, has been recently restored and developed as the Raymond VI Gardens, a long series of gardens culminating in a terrace overlooking the Garonne. From this point, we can enjoy a panoramic view over the river, the daring Catalan Bridge (1910-1913) and the town.

The Gué du Bazacle

The Abattoirs:
Centre d'art moderne et contemporain

The old slaughter house buildings (Abattoirs) built by Urbain Vitry between 1828 and 1831 and now entirely renovated, house the Toulouse and Midi-Pyrenees regional modern and contemporary art collections. Almost 2000 20th century works of art enrich this art center, representing the different currents of style that have flowed through modern art among which, for example, figures the celebrated "14th of July theatre backcloth" by Picasso. Exhibitions, meeting rooms, a multimedia room, an auditorium and a café-restaurant, are all planned for, at the Abattoirs.

FROM TOP TO BOTTOM

Saint-Pierre-des-Cuisines; Church interior transformed into an auditorium.

16th century ramparts near the Abattoirs.

The Abattoirs, Centre d'art moderne et contemporain.

The Chaussée du Bazacle and the Hospice de la Grave.

**The Couvent des Chartreux buildings
were requisitioned in the revolutionary era
as an arsenal for the Army of the Pyrenees.
Only a portion remains of the arcature of the main cloister,
which was once neighboured by small houses
which served as lodgings for the monks,
permitting them to lead a life of solitude
in the framework of their community.
The site, nicely renovated and planted,
is one of the most pleasant parks in the center of the city.**

Detail of the panel from the Ponts-Jumeaux.

The Chaussée du Bazacle recalls the old river ford which permitted the crossing of the river at any time. On the right bank were the mills of Bazacle as cited by Rabelais, owned by stockholders known as "bettors", from the end of the 12th century on. The architectural remains of this area may be visited during special events organized by the National Electric Company (EDF), which now owns the land. The visit is highly recommended, as it also allows access to a special site above the river where a fish lift allows a view of the fauna of the Garonne. Sunset over the town gives a Venetian aspect to this view.

The Quartier Saint-Cyprien

The waterfront façade of the Quartier Saint-Cyprien is marked by two large buildings, the Hospice de la Grave and the Hôtel-Dieu Saint-Jacques, and by the large Prairie des Filtres a very pleasant place to walk overlooked by the Cours Dillon planted with plane trees. This neighbourhood, frequently flooded despite the construction of dykes in the 18th century, owes its name to an ancient chapel dedicated to Saint Cyprien, which once stood in the area. As the gateway to Gascony, it emerged as a center for customs and trade in the Middle Ages. The activity along the district's main artery –the Rue de la République leading to the Place Intérieure

Saint-Cyprien – should not make the visitor forget the discreet charm of streets which still give it the atmosphere of a village. Several fine houses, from the 16th to the 19th century, survived the dreadful flood of 1875 and even the town planning of the second half of the 20th century which was no less dreadful. The Couvent des Feuillants with its 17th century church and cloister houses the Grand Seminaire; the Centre Municipal de l'Affiche with its permanent graphic arts and postcard exhibitions, situated on the Allées Charles-de-Fitte is open to the public. These exhibitions use, as their theme, images which acted as milestones in the memories of our childhood and those of our grand-parents. ("the bicycle", "the circus" Toulouse-Lautrec"…)

The Hospice de la Grave

Built at the water's edge at the end of the 12th century, the Hospice de la Grave housed the elderly, the incurably ill, abandoned children and "immoral" women. Its design, redone in the 17th century, was respected until the 20th century. Each independent building was reserved for a specific category of patients, organized around interior courts equipped with wells, where the plants necessary for the feeding and care of the ill were cultivated. Just before the Revolution, the hospice saw the addition of

Saint-Nicolas (14th century) is the district church of Toulouse. The architecture is typical of the southern Gothic style with its single nave, its chapels set between buttresses, its wide projecting roof and its small external windows.

the neighbouring buildings of the Couvent des Dames de la Porte (Clarisses)- replaced in 1835 by a colonnaded neo-classic building conceived in the Doric Order- reaching to the Rue Réclusane and to the 16th century ramparts. The Chapelle de la Grave, whose construction began in 1750, saw its share of tribulations; its wood foundations gradually needed to be replaced by others in concrete and its dome, whose copper roof, tarnished by oxydisation and restored several times, elegantly breaks the austerity of the façades along the Garonne.

The Église Saint-Nicolas

The first chapel of the neighbourhood, dedicated to Saint Cyprien, was one of the many buildings which disappeared without leaving a trace. The re-dedication in favor of Saint Nicolas placed this outlying district under the protection of the patron saint of sailors and drowning victims. The church was rebuilt in the 14th century, as shown by the keystones decorated with coats of arms, leaves and historical figures (including Saint Paul). The steeple was completed, with its upper levels ornamented by the traditional cowled arches, at the end of the 14th century (its spire was rebuilt in 1787).

Inside can be seen a reredos, perhaps the most beautiful in Toulouse, created according to the drawings of J-B. Despax (1788), who also created the paintings (with the death and apotheosis of Saint Nicolas in the center). Different-colored marbles, gilding and painting are associated in a single baroque theatrical movement intended more to affect worshipers' hearts than their minds.

The sculpted stonework of the portal, which is believed to date from the second half of the 15th century, is unfinished. The finesse and care used in the creation of the sculptures is impressive; vegetal ornaments, small animals, etc. Six of the lateral niches received statues. Four of them, dating from the 15th century, reached the 20th century in decent condition but are currently in a poor state. The statues of Saint Cyprian and Saint Nicholas were created by the sculptor Rouzet (1863). In the tympanum, the sculpture of the Adoration of the Magi has been replaced by a moulded duplicate. The original has been placed in one of the chapels, where one can conveniently see it and appreciate the quality of the expressions, imprinted with a softness and pathos particular to the late Middle Ages.

The Hôtel-Dieu Saint-Jacques

The Hôtel-Dieu Saint-Jacques presents a vast brick façade along the waterfront. It embraces the outlet of the last support of the covered bridge which linked the Port de la Daurade to the Quartier Saint-Cyprien. This vast establishment is the heir to two hospitals, the Hôpital Sainte-Marie mentioned in the first third of the 12th century and the Hôpital Nouvel founded in 1235. Run by the fraternity of Saint James beginning in the 13th century, it took its final form in the 16th century when some thirty charitable institutions were linked to it.

At the outlet of the Pont-Neuf, three 17th century buildings open onto a French garden. To the East, a double flight of stairs marks the location of the former Rue aux Herbes, which prolonged the covered bridge. To the right of the entrance is the tower where abandoned children were left. In the interior is located the Salle Saint-Jacques, where portraits of benefactors were often hung (the wooden ceiling dates from the 17th century), and the chapel. Neo-classic in its present form, the chapel replaced a mediaeval structure of which only a few examples of stone work remain together with a gemelled window. (visible from the small interior courtyard) The building which clo-

ses off the garden contains the vast Saint-Lazare common room, also known as the columned-room. The Hôtel-Dieu Saint-Jacques currently houses the local hospital administration, which is very interested in the building's renovation. The creation of a museum of the History of Medicine, an offshoot of the Toulouse Society of Medicine, Surgery and Pharmacy (one of several scientific societies whose seat is located in the Hôtel d'Assézat), is entirely due to the efforts of Professor Jean-Charles Auvergnat. The four exhibition rooms which contain the history of 19th century pharmacy, illustrations, drawings, old medical instruments and various objects, relates the story of seven centuries of Toulouse medicine and details the progress and the ideas that motivated those involved in this science.

The Château d'eau (water tower)

The water tower was built in 1823. Its perfect design allowed the city to be supplied with water until 1860. After more than a century of abandonment, and thanks to the will and the obstinacy of the great photographer Jean Dieuzaide, it has been restored (the machinery is still visible) and transformed into a municipal photography gallery, one of the best-known in Europe. The exhibitions

View of the town; the Pont-Neuf and the Quais seen from the Pont Saint-Pierre.

change each month, attracting large numbers of visitors. A second gallery and an archive have been installed under the arches of the adjoining Pont-Neuf.

The Pont-Neuf and the Quais

The strength of the Pont-Neuf has defied the centuries and the waters of the river which carried away so many constructions, like the Roman aqueduct bridge (upstream) and the Pont de la Daurade (12th to 17th centuries) downstream. Like so many other "Pont-Neuf" in France, it is now one of the oldest bridges in the city. Its construction took more than half a century, beginning in 1544, and some of the greatest architects, for example Thomas Bachelier, took part in the work.

The visitor standing on this bridge discovers the city from behind the wharves built under the impetus of Archbishop Loménie de Bienne at the end of the 18th century. The layout clearly shows the links which unite the city with the river, with the wharves, the ports and the mooring rings for the boats embedded in the strong brick walls. Old views of the city, seen in postcards and engravings, bring to life the incessant movement which reigned at the time; today, it is a place for pleasant walks and, during the warm

weather, it becomes Toulouse's "beach". The great masses of the Église des Jacobins, of the Église de la Daurade and the Église de la Dalbade, their towers shooting above the crowded rooftops, invite us to continue our discoveries. From this bridge, one can also see, towards the south, the slopes of Pech David and the old town of Toulouse, where formerly a pre-Roman oppidum existed. In addition, on fine bright days one can see the Pyrenees mountain range where the Garonne has its source on Spanish soil.

The Jacobins

The Dominican order was founded in Toulouse in 1215 by Saint Dominic and was recognized in 1217 by Pope Honorious III. The monks moved into a monastery on Rue Saint-Rome in 1216 and then acquired in 1229 (the same year that the University was created) the land where a much larger conventual building would gradually be built. The church, designed with a rectangular layout and a straight chevet and covered only by a framework, began construction in 1229. It occupied the area which is taken up by the first five bays of the current nave. This church, lower than the current building, reflected the spirit of poverty of the first Dominicans. It was divided into two

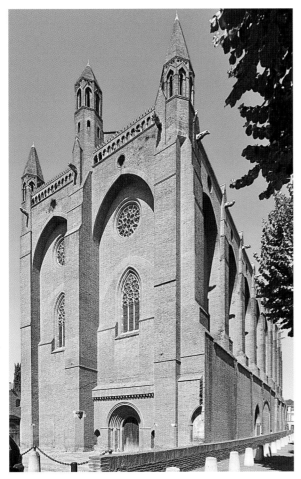

Western façade of the Église des Jacobins.
OPPOSITE PAGE **Interior, Église des Jacobins.**
FOLLOWING DOUBLE PAGE
The famous "palm tree" roof of the Église des Jacobins.

ces, donated by Cardinal Godin between 1323 and 1324.

In 1368, a major event occurred; the pope of Avignon Urban V expressed his wish that the body of Saint Thomas Aquinas (who died in Fosanova, Italy, in 1274) be buried in what he described as "the most beautiful and the most splendid" place, and he chose the Dominican church of Toulouse, with whose "grandeur and magnificence" he was familiar. On January 29, 1369, the body of the "Angelic Doctor" was brought to the church with great pomp and ceremony.

On October 22, 1385, the church was finally completed and was dedicated to Saint Thomas Aquinas. Its grandiose and original design made it a masterpiece of gothic architecture in Southern France. It measures 80 meters long, 20 meters wide and its 22-meter-high columns are among the highest raised by Gothic architecture. One of the columns, slightly wider than the others, supports 22 ribs radiating from it to the vault like the leaves of a palm tree.

In the 19th century, under military occupation, a one-meter-thick embankment placed the floor of the church at the same level as the ground outside. The church was divided vertically by the installation of two additional floors. Prosper Mérimée, visiting the site in 1840, denounced this vandalism which had disfigured the church.

With the arrival of the era of restorations, painted décor also reappeared. The walls were painted to resemble stone, the stones making the ribs were painted alternately red and green, the coat of arms of Cardinal Godin was painted on the reverse side of the façade and friezes graced the entry to the chapels. The stained-glass windows of the chevet were reconstituted between 1923 and 1930 based on a simulation of the décor of the opening in the wall corresponding to the steeple. The stained-glass in the nave were created in 1956 by Max Ingrand, who respected the chromatic design of the original windows conserved in the rose windows of the façade. Warm colors such as red and yellow dominated the southern end, while cooler tints such as blue and green were reserved for the northern nave.

The octagonal steeple rose alongside the church and was completed in 1298. Its four levels were decorated on each side by gemelled windows and topped by cowled arches. The steeple is crowned by an elegant arcature with small columns and capitals in marble. It was originally topped by a 15-meter spire, constructed of a wood frame and covered with lead, which was destroyed during the Revolution under the pretext that it was an outrage against the principle of Equality. The cloister was built from 1307 to 1310. The double marble columns support capitals whose motifs are generally plants. In the north-eastern corner of the courtyard can be seen the remains of the wash basin. Only the western and the northern

bays of unequal width, the southern one of which was used for sermons while the northern one was occupied by the monks' choir. The black marble tiles in the current floor, show the foundation of the previous building, whose only vestige is the Romanesque portal situated on the western façade.

From 1244 to 1253, the lower part of the current chevet was added to the eastern portion of this sober building. The building was raised and vaulted between 1275 and 1292. It was separated into two equal parts by three cylindrical columns, while high windows provided abundant light. On February 2, 1292, Bertrand de Montaigu, the Moissac abbot, celebrated the first mass on the altar of the chapel dedicated to the Virgin Mary. The contrast must have been great between the first church, low and unadorned, and this majestic chevet. The nave was later remodelled along the lines of the chevet, thanks to a donation of 4,000 gold pie-

The Basilique de la Daurade (18th century) overlooks the former Port de la Daurade, nowadays very pleasantly developed and suitable for relaxation.

Neo-classical façade (19th century) of the Basilique de la Daurade.

galleries (minus two arcades) survived in their authentic state; the rest were redone between 1960 and 1970 by the re-use of marble elements originating from the cloister of the Église des Jacobins or similar cloisters, discovered by Maurice Prin who has played a vital role in saving and restoring this ancient monastery.

The chapter house, finished in 1301, owes its existence to the generosity of a priest, Arnaud Vilar, whose coat of arms is inscribed on several keystones. The room's ceiling is made up of six vaults on intersecting ribs. In the center, two slim prismatic marble columns carry the weight of the arches which cut into each other, giving a lighter, airy feel. A chapel formed by a vaulted seven-sided apse shelters an altar, painted in bright colors to resemble stone. In the 17th century, portraits of illustrious members of the order were painted in the room. The chapter, or assembly of the religious, was held in this room, which also received professors and their assistants from the mediaeval University.

The Chapelle Saint-Antonin, completed in 1341, was built thanks to Dominique Grima, the bishop of Pamiers and formerly a friar at the monastery. Designed as a funeral chapel, it held the sepulchres of the religious and the canons of the Cathédrale de Pamiers, and, in its center, that of its founder. The chapel is built in southern style as regards to its proportions, but also as regards to the large wall surfaces and vaults which invite rich decoration. In the vault and in the medallions can be seen the second vision of the Apocalypse (God the Father giving blessings, Jesus on his knees, surrounded by the tetramorph; Christ holding the book of Seven Seals; busts of the 24 Old Men), and high on the walls, angels bearing incense burners together with musicians. On the reverse side of the façade, Saint Dominic, Saint Peter of Verona and Saint Anthony were depicted. The many episodes of the legend of Saint Anthony are traced on the side walls of the chapel in a series of trefoiled arches.

The refectory (1301-1303) is a vast room measuring 50 meters in length, with a wooden ceiling in the form of a ship's hull mounted on apertured arches and painted to simulate the appearance of stone.

The Daurade

Named for the gold-based mosaics which ornamented it, the first Église Sainte-Marie la Daurade disappeared forever in 1761. Mystery continues to surround the origins, whether antique or early Christian, of this irregular polygon. Drawings, descriptions and vestiges of marble sculptures give an idea of it structure, of the splendor of its decor, and of the date of its origin, which is often cited as the 5th century. The interior, enlivened by three rows of niches flanked by columns (several fine examples of which complete with their capitals, are in the Musée Saint-Raymond), was covered with precious mosaics. Higher up were scenes from the Childhood of Christ, while towards the middle, the Saviour and the Virgin Mary were depicted surrounded by archangels, apostles and characters from the Old Testament who continue to appear lower on the wall. The cupola was pierced by a high rounded opening.

The center of a monastery mentioned in 844, the church became the priory of Moissac in 1077. Renovation work was undertaken, and a nave was built, transforming the early Christian building into the choir of the new structure; a Romanesque cloister spread out its galleries and its chapter house to the south of the church, accompanied by monastic buildings. In the 17th century, all of the buildings, in very poor condition, came under the ownership of the Maurists. The vaults of the nave had to be demolished in 1759. A new dome, placed over the choir in 1760, worsened the cracking of the old walls. The decision was taken to demolish both the church and the surrounding buildings; the cloister was left intact until 1811. A first attempt at reconstruction, in 1765, was interrupted because the design did not fit in with the planned alignment of the docks. The current edifice began to rise in 1772. After a halt during the Revolution, during which the buildings were converted into cotton and then tobacco manufacturing facilities, the church was finally dedicated in 1836. The colonnade and the pediment of its façade (1877-1888) followed by that of the Palais des Arts (1892) completed the transformation of this former Benedictine monastery.

Hôtel-Dieu Saint-Jacques: Classical façade, riverside.
An arch from the former mediaeval Pont de la Daurade still exists, projecting over the river.

The interior of the church continues the solemn order of the Roman churches of the 17th century, with its Corinthian pilasters, its over-lowered vaults and its transept with semi-circular wings. The painter J. Roques from Toulouse created seven paintings for the choir. The southern wing of the transept houses, in an enamelled terra-cotta receptacle, a widely venerated statue of the Black Virgin dating from 1807. The statue was created after the memory of the 14th century original, which was burned during the Revolution, and represents the Marian piety, which has existed in this spot perhaps as far back as the council of Ephesus in 431 A.D. The basilica still possesses a fine Treasury where examples of the goldsmith's sacred art exist side by side with a curious canvas from either the 16th or 17th century depicting the mystical olive press.

The Quartier commerçant (shopping district)

The shopping district is concentrated between the Rue Saint-Rome and the Rue des Changes on the one hand and the wharves on the other. It is characterized by the long shape of the blocks and the narrowness of the streets. Here are mixed together humble houses and mansions, built after the fire of 1463, which have left the street façade to the stores and have reserved the inner courtyards for themselves. The very names of the streets recall the intense activity which took place here during the Middle Ages; Rue des Changes (money changers), Rue Peyrolières (boilermakers), Rue Tripière (butchers) where N° 12 to 14 have recently been refurbished as a museum of Trade Guilds. We also must evoke the pastel plant, which was one of the major factors in Toulouse's growth during the second half of the 15th and the first half of the 16th centuries. This plant, after long and careful preparation, produced a dye which was the only one, until the appearance of indigo, to provide indelible blues. Several merchants scented the commercial potential of the process and found the necessary financing to put the product on the international market. The Assézat, Bernuy, Cheverry, Delfau and Boysson families demonstrated their financial success by the construction of prestigious homes in the very heart of the neighbourhoods where they had developed their businesses. The arrival of indigo from India, at a time when the pastel harvest was substandard, combined with the Protestant conflicts, put an end to this golden age.

Hôtels particuliers (private mansions)

The first mansions, built around the end of the 15th century, are particularly notable for their modest dimensions. The mansion of P. Delfau (20 Rue de la Bourse), built before 1500, is typical; the street façade opens onto the large boutique arch, recently restored with its fine vaulted ceiling and its hallway leading to a first court. A second building, parallel to the first, looks out on a garden, the winding staircase is situated on a corner of the building, a small corbelled tower provides access to the attic and, from there, to a terrace. Large 16th century mansions were decorated by a complete set of ornaments for the entry court (the street façade often remained austere). This is the case for the mansion that Jean de Bernuy had built in the first years of the 16th century, in the present Rue Gambetta. The oldest parts, the façade and the second court, still show gothic design. Bernuy entrusted Louis Privat with the work on the first court, all in sculpted stone, which was finished in 1530. On the reverse side of the façade, two arches mark the ground floor and three mark the first floor. A large arch, perilously over-lowered, decorated with coffers, supports the first floor of the perpendicular wing, lit by two large

lattice-work windows. The exuberance of the decorations, which bears the mark of various designs that originated in northern Italy or the Loire region and then were reinterpreted, displayed the power of Jean de Bernuy, who was so rich that he guaranteed the ransom payment of François I. (In return, the king visited his mansion in 1533…).

But the Renaissance had entered a new phase in Toulouse; the desire for classical composition emerged, architectural treatises circulated and were discussed in

Interior court, Hôtel de Bernuy.

The Hôtel d'Astorg and Saint-Germain.

PRECEDING DOUBLE PAGE
The Hôtel d'Assézat (16th century) is a veritable Renaissance palace. The north and east wings are articulated around a monumental stairway terminated by two terraces and surmounted by a skylight on an octagonal base.

Loggia of the Hôtel d'Assézat.

humanist circles. It is in this context that the Hôtel d'Assézat was born, with the contribution of the architect Nicolas Bachelier. Two groups of buildings are situated around a vast court and articulated around a majestic staircase. Their three levels, whose height decreases at each level, are each decorated with regularly placed windows framed by columns, whose capitals are, successively, Doric, Ionic and Corinthian. The window frames and the columns are in stone, and their light tones mixed with that of the brick, create a certain feeling of fantasy, adding to the exceptional harmony of the whole. On the back of the façade facing the street, a portico surmounted by a gallery raises its four rhythmic arches on columns bearing a frieze. The fourth side of the court was constituted by a common wall, which was enlivened by a corbelled gallery supported by flattened arches.

This Renaissance palace has housed, since the end of the 19th century, the city's academic and intellectual societies, the most ancient of which is the Académie des Jeux Floraux, the heir to the Consistoire du Gai Savoir founded in 1323 by the seven troubadours. But mention must also be made of the Académie des Sciences, Inscriptions and Belles Lettres, which dates back to the 17th century and

House decorated with caryatids, n° 28 Rue des Marchands (1830's).

the Société Archéologique du Midi de la France, founded in 1831. Their archives, libraries and collections form a considerable richness of resources. The Bemberg foundation has more recently found a choice setting to house its collections, essentially composed of prints, which cover a long period from the Renaissance to the 20th century.

The Garonnette

Before exploring the Rue de la Dalbade, the visitor should stand on the Pont de Tounis (1515-1516), which spanned the Garonnette, a natural arm of the Garonne, which dried up in the middle of the 20th century. On one side, can be seen the picturesque clusters of houses and the beautiful outlet into the Garonne, while on the other side are the garden façades of old buildings. The Hôtel Le Masuyer and the Institut Catholique (formerly the Couvent de Sainte-Claire du Salin) form an imposing architectural ensemble.

The Dalbade

Seen from far, the church presents its façade topped by three small brick towers and, to the rear, its square steeple giving it the look of a defensive tower. This steeple which, since the 16th century, had raised its quadrangular mass,

inspired by the bell tower of Sainte-Cécile d'Albi, and topped by a spire more than 80 meters above the ground (the highest in the town) collapsed in 1926 carrying the church vaults with it in its fall and destroying numerous works of art. Some of the thirty or forty busts sculpted in the 16th century by Bachelier and his students to adorn the steeple were saved in the ruins. Also saved were four splendid relief sculptures from the main reredos, which can now be viewed at the Musée des Augustins.

According to tradition, the Église de la Dalbade ("the White Church") replaced a chapel founded in the seventh century by Saint-Germier. As a Marian sanctuary which was the property of the Daurade, it was rebuilt for the first time at the end of the 12th century. But when a fire ravaged the neighbourhood and the church in 1442, it was restored and most probably enlarged. It was the age when the district took on the general appearance it has today, with the arrival of prosperous bourgeois and aristocrats. The work done on the church was undoubtedly insufficient, as an entire reconstruction was begun at the end of the 15th century. The five-sided choir was built from 1480 to 1490, followed by the steeple, the single nave flanked by chapels, between buttresses and finally

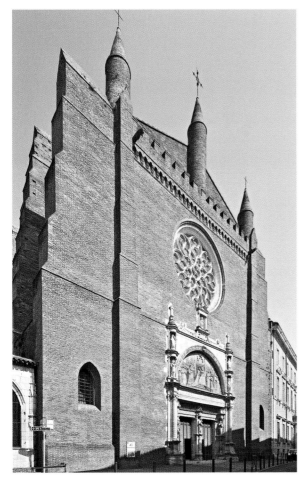

the portal in sculpted stone, recently cleaned. The portal demonstrates the spirit of the years 1530-1540: if the concept remains gothic (with the presence of a tympanum, decorated in 1878 by Gaston Virebent with a reproduction in enamelled ceramic of the Crowning of the Virgin Mary by Fra Angelico and a pier), the mouldings, the decorative repertoire in Spanish Baroque, the columned candelabra, all without doubt belong to the Renaissance. The huge and flamboyant rose window set in the brick wall is the most dynamic stone interlacement ever to have been installed in a Toulouse church.

The Palais des chevaliers de Saint-Jean de Jérusalem ou de Malte

These brilliant knights, with their aura of eastern prestige, took up residence here around the year 1115 and on into the 12th and 13th centuries. They built a whole architectural group of buildings with a Romanesque Église Saint-Jean whose portal, complete with capitals,(recognised from several drawings) was still visible in the 19th century from the Rue de la Dalbade. As heirs to the holdings of the Templars, they founded the grand priory of Toulouse in 1315, in this early monastery. Despite its almost total

demolition, some traces of the southern wall of the church still exist against which some tombs in funerary niches can still be seen. A gothic sarcophagus with a quadrilobate decoration which is in the Musée des Augustins, originated from one of these niches. Two new niches have just been discovered with an interesting recumbant female figure and some excellent mediaeval murals. In the 17th century the Hospitallers asked Jean-Pierre Rivalz to mount a veritable Roman Palace, between the Dalbade and Saint-Jean at the place where the priory stood in the Middle Ages. The façade lined up with a portal, in the archway of which was included a fine wrought-iron springer, was lengthened in the 19th century to be identical with a second portal after the Église Saint-Jean was levelled.

The Rue de la Dalbade

Almost nothing in this street leaves the passer-by indifferent. What the façades do not reveal must be searched for in the courtyards. Such is the case for the Hôtel de Bruni (a 16th century stairway tower), the Hôtel de la Mamye (a two-bayed façade with three floors of galleries, from the 16th century) and the Hôtel d'Aldéguier (a courtyard from the early 18th century). In marked contrast is the Hôtel

Detail and elevation
facing the court of the Hôtel de la Mamye
(31, Rue de la Dalbade), from the 16th century.
The three superimposed galleries correspond to
the three classical orders (Doric, Ionic and Corinthian)
found at the Hôtel d'Assézat.

Façade of the "Hôtel de Pierre."

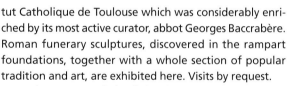

FOLLOWING PAGE
Portal of the "Hôtel de Pierre" courtyard.
Telamon statue by Nicolas Bachelier (16th century).

which dominates the passer-by with its vain façade which gained it the name of the "Hôtel de Pierre" ("mansion of stone"). Around 1535, Jean de Bagis bought several parcels of land and asked N. Bachelier to build his mansion, of which the northern and western wings remain. In the western wing, a magnificent portal, whose crown is carried by two statues, provides access to an Italian staircase. François de Clary remodelled the buildings to the south and to the east in the 17th century and built on the street the celebrated stone façade decorated with relief sculptures and sequences of colossal pilasters, the capitals of which are ornamented with a mixture of eagles and acanthus leaves. This façade was "completed" in 1857.

The Rue de la Dalbade continues towards the Place du Parlement and Place du Salin by means of the Rue de la Fonderie. This name recalls the changing of the Couvent des Clarisses into a cannon foundry in the 19th century: currently the Headquarters of the Institut Catholique de Toulouse, the convent has preserved its façade and the portal of its gothic chapel facing the street. On descending to the bottom of the main courtyard "the Passage des Trinqueballes", the eloquent remains of the wall added in the 3rd century along the banks of the Garonne can be seen. Situated here is the Musée archéologique de l'Insti-

tut Catholique de Toulouse which was considerably enriched by its most active curator, abbot Georges Baccrabère. Roman funerary sculptures, discovered in the rampart foundations, together with a whole section of popular tradition and art, are exhibited here. Visits by request.

On the western side (N°7) the Place du Parlement comes into view. A segment of the ancient rampart wall from the 1st century has been included in its elevation. Built on to this façade are the remains of the house that Pierre Seila gave (in 1215) to Saint Dominique before the brothers constructed their first monastery in the Rue Saint-Rome. This building underwent many modifications: Inquisition Hall, a nunnery of the Marie-Réparatrice Order and today is the annexe of the Institut Catholique. This building, full of historical memories, is now regularly opened to the public. The chapel, constructed in the middle of the 17th century, is decorated with a coffered ceiling embellished by Brother Balthazar Moncornet with scenes of the life of Saint Dominique.

The Parlement (Parliament) and the Palais de justice (Law Court)

The Languedoc Parliament met permanently in Toulouse beginning in 1443. The first of the provincial Parliaments,

Façade overlooking the court of the "Hôtel de Pierre" (17th C). In the sculpted decorations ancient marble slabs were incorporated.

its organization was slowly improved. The Grande Chambre had two presidents (and a third beginning in 1460), and its work was prepared by the Chambre des Enquêtes. Beginning in the 16th century, the Chambre des Tournelles took responsibility for criminal affaires and the Chambre des Vacations (which functioned during vacation periods) and the Chambre des Requêtes were added on to the Parliament. In 1519, 30 councillors worked in the Parliament; by the 17th century their number had increased to 150, accompanied by a crowd of magistrates, lawyers and clerks. Gradually venality and nepotism exercised their effects.

The Parliament was seated in the Château Narbonnais, (the former residence of the Counts of Toulouse), attached in part to the southern gateway of the ancient City and possibly also to what are now the remains of a triumphal Roman arch, recognized from a 16th century drawing. The buildings were largely demolished in the 16th century. The architect J-P Laffon rebuilt the Cour d'Appel between 1828 and 1833; today it forms the Palais de Justice along with the Tribunal de Grande Instance (1845-52) and the Cour d'Assises (around 1840). Nonetheless, memories of the Parliament remain despite its dissolution in 1790,

including the Salon Doré (15th and 17th century decoration), the chapel and the Salon d'Hercule (17th century carved wood ceiling, representing the twelve labours of the Greco-Roman hero), and the Grande Chambre whose ceiling, painted in the 15th century, has recently been uncovered. According to archaeological research of which much is expected towards improving our knowledge of the history of Toulouse, this building should contribute to what is already known about the architecture of that time. The members of Parliament saw their financial position increase at the same time as their appetite for splendor. Their urban dwellings are there to bear witness, as are their properties bought by them in the surrounding countryside. Their mansions fit the definition given by the architect d'Aviler, at the end of the 17th century (quoted by P. Mesplé), that is "a distinctive house inhabited by a person of quality."

The Rue Pharaon and Rue des Filatiers

The Rue Pharaon starts at the former Royal Treasury in the Place du Salin, onto which faces the Palais de Justice (Law Court) and where can the building from the close of the Middle Ages can still be found, today transformed into a

**Tablet over the doorway to the stairway tower
of the Hôtel du Vieux-Raisin (16th century);
36, Rue du Languedoc.**

**Lodgings of the Hôtel Dahus (15th century)
and the Tour de Tournoër (16th century).
Other parts of the Hôtel Dahus
are to be found in the Hôtel du Vieux-Raisin.**

Protestant temple. Following on from the Place des Carmes (the large convent disappeared from here in 1808) the road continues into Rue des Filatiers. All along these two roads and also in the adjacent streets, lovers of Toulouse will make many discoveries. The Rue Pharaon for example. The parish of the Spaniards was established at N°20, in the Église Saint-Antoine du Salin (façade by J-P Rivalz), juxtaposed with a small classical cloister. In the courtyard of N°21, the finely wrought gothic door of the tower of the Hôtel Rolle; N° 47 consists of the still intact mansion belonging to Jean Marvejol, merchant and municipal magistrate who lived here during the first third of the 17th century. Its shop, its mirande windows, its lateral corridor giving onto the interior courtyard where the wooden galleries and the well have been preserved, still exists. At N° 9 Rue des Filatiers it is imperative to pause in front of the goldsmith Elie Gerauld's house with its carved wooden window façade (1577). The Calas mansion at N° 50 is not to be missed. During the night of the 12th to the 13th of October 1761, the body of Marc-Antoine Calas was discovered here. He had been hung. His father Jean Calas, falsely accused of his murder, was condemned by the Parliament and put to the wheel alive on the Place Saint-Georges.

This infamous judicial error, committed in a climate of religious intolerance, provoked, as one knows, Voltaire's intervention which in 1765 led to the rehabilitation of Jean Calas. The road opens out onto the pretty Place de la Trinité where a 19th century fountain babbles gently.

The Rue du Languedoc and Rue Ozenne

These two streets, laid out at the end of the 19th and beginning of the 20th centuries, destroyed the links which united the neighbourhoods of the Carmes and Saint-Étienne. Their recent creation must be taken into account in order to understand what remains of the Hôtel Bérenguier-Maynier (commonly called the Hôtel du Vieux-Raisin), the Hôtel Dahus, the Hôtel Baderon-Maussac and the Hôtel Potier-Laterasse as well as the influence of that great humanist Jean de Pins.

Rue Ozenne remains an impressive example of 15th century public architecture, as shown by the Hôtel Dahus, a tall building crowned by false machicolations from which emerge gargoyles. In the 16th century, the next owner undertook the construction of the hexagonal tower, which was completed by the parliamentary councillor Guillaume de Tournoër.

FROM TOP TO BOTTOM

View of the Église and Clocher des Augustins, seen from the Great cloister.

The galleries of the Great cloister of the Augustins house gothic sculptures of which this set of gargoyles, originating from the Église des Cordeliers, destroyed in 1874.

OPPOSITE PAGE

The Jesuit apothecary, from the Noviciat des Jésuites (which was located on Place de la Daurade), preserved at the Musée Paul-Dupuy.

The Hôtel du Vieux-Raisin has preserved part of the lodgings belonging to Pierre Dahus. Between 1515 and 1528, construction began on the central building, the beginning of the two wings and the two staircase towers, which were completed in the 16th century. Here, two periods of the Renaissance are expressed, the first one appearing in the initial construction with the decoration of the doors and windows with pilasters decorated with candelabra and surmounted by friezes of foliage. The second one is manifested in the portico and the framing of the windows created by the new owner Jean Burnet, where the caryatids recall the vigor of Nicolas Bachelier's work on the Hôtel de Pierre. Not far away, overlooking the present Rue Philippe-Féral, the Italian catholic community uses a private chapel from the 16th century; Notre-Dame de Nazareth. Little known, it deserves however a few moments of attention for its architecture, its 16th century stained-glass window, depicting the Nativity, and its remarkable 17th century wood sculptures.

The Musée Paul-Dupuy

Installed in a 17th century mansion, the museum was built around the collections assembled by Paul Dupuy in the first half of the 20th century. Augmented by several donations and large purchases, it is one of the greatest French museums of decorative art. The clock collection (donated by Gélis) is exceptional. Earthenware art, the arts of glass, ivory, bronze, silver, gold and clothing together with the Salon de Musique evoke the art of living of past centuries. Amongst the ancient measuring instruments can be found the extremely rare Abu Bekr astrolabe (year 613 of the Hegira: 1216-1217). The 17th century Jesuit apothecary is perfectly at home here. One can still admire the "Cor de Roland" (an ivory horn from the 11th century) and Saint Exupère's enamelled reliquary originating from the former Saint-Sernin Treasury, together with the embroidered Cordelier altar facing, decorated with medaillons showing scenes from the Gospel and the life of Saint Francis. The museum also houses a large set of mediaeval and modern coins, and an extraordinary rich collection of drawings and engravings, periodically put on display. Numerous graphic documents ensure that the Musée Paul Dupuy cannot be ignored by those who are interested in the iconography of the whole of the Languedoc region.

The Musée des Augustins: Musée des Beaux-Arts

Toulouse's municipal Musée des Beaux-Arts (painting and sculpture) is located in the former Couvent des Augustins. It was in its vast church, constructed between the beginning of the 14th century and the beginning of the 16th century that the "Provisional Museum of the Midi of the République" established, from 1794 onwards, art collections from the Capitole, the Parliament, the churches and the monasteries, the emigrant hostels and learned societies, along with all other antiquities "capable of serving in the future for the history of the commune". The cloister (finished in 1396) provides access to the sacristy (14th century), the Chapelle Notre-Dame de Pitié (1341) and to the chapter house (14th to 15th centuries), all of which

Musée des Augustins: detail of Christ descendu de la Croix, by Nicolas Tournier (1590-1639), one of the best examples of the Caravaggio school.

offer an architecture of great quality. The surroundings are perfectly suitable for the presentation of gothic sculptures; funerary works (a remarkable recumbent statue from the tomb of Guillaume Durant, the sarcophagus of Chevalier Hugues de Palais, the elegantly engraved plaque to Marquesia de Linars), an outstanding set of statues (around 1340) from the Chapelle de Rieux showing two figures (recumbent and kneeling, offering his chapel) of Jean Tissendier its founding bishop, a statue universally known as "Nostre-Dame de Grasse" (15th century, originating from the Église des Jacobins). The famous set of Romanesque sculptures is displayed in the western part of the cloister in a late 19th century massive building replacing the 14th century refectory, which was destroyed in order to allow the construction of the Rue d'Alsace-Lorraine. Wreckage from the vandalism, which ravaged Toulouse in the 19th century, the capitals of the cloisters of Saint-Sernin, the Daurade and Saint-Étienne and their great relief sculptures (the extraordinary marble panel originating from Saint-Sernin representing the Zodiac signs of the Lion and the Ram) evoke all the lost 12th century monuments, the iconographic inventions and the

stylistic mutations which they held. Also in the collection are many other equally remarkable Romanesque works from Narbonne, Saint-Gaudens, Lombez and Saint-Rustice. A very important series of engraved mediaeval lapidary inscriptions (from the 11th to the 16th centuries) can be seen in an adjacent gallery.

The church has been devoted to religious art: 16th and 18th century sculptures (relief panels by Nicolas Bachelier for the Dalbade reredos) and paintings from the 14th and 18th centuries (two aspects of Christ from Cardinal Godin originating from the Jacobins, Rubens' crucifixion, works from the Caravaggio School by Nicolas Tournier). The permanent painting exhibition continues on the first and second floors of the 19th century building: Flemish, Dutch, Italian, French schools, Toulouse artists (Antoine Rivalz, Joseph Roques) and southern artists (Ingres). In the Salon Rouge the 19th century works (Corot, Courbet, Delacroix, Constant, Laurens) are hung in the manner of traditional galleries of paintings. The little 17th century cloister with its beautiful 17th and 18th terracotta sculptures (Marc Arcis, Lucas) should round off the visit.

In the Hôtel d'Ulmo courtyard (Rue Ninau),
a flight of steps topped by a very elegant canopy provides
access to a stairway with straight banisters (16th century).

The Hôtel de Lafage, built in the middle of the 18th century,
forms the eastern side of the Place Saint-Georges,
one of the permanently lively areas of Toulouse.

The Quartier Saint-Étienne

Beyond the Rue d'Alsace-Lorraine and the Rue Ozenne, in the direction of Saint-Étienne, stretches a neighbourhood rich in 16th, 17th and 18th century houses and mansions. The Rue Croix-Baragnon includes a series of homes of surprising quality. A mediaeval house, early 14th century, has preserved, despite repeated renovations, a set of five gemelled windows, linked by a frieze showing animals flanking ceremonial shields. Its gothic door has recently been removed and restored. Further on, the classical Hôtel de Castellane (18th century) faces the street with its monumental portal surmounted by terracotta lions. The façade of the Hôtel Bonnefoy (renovated in 1729-1730) still bears the trace of medieval gemelled windows, and in its court, rises a beautiful gothic tower (1513). A number of balconies are made of forged iron and date from the 18th century; Bernard Ortet created the balconies at the Hôtel Bonfontan (N°41). The neighbouring streets are equally rich in such sights. For example, the Rue Ninau includes the Hôtel d'Ulmo. On the street, a high wall, pierced by a large carriage entrance and surmounted by a passageway, links the two wings of the great brick building. The main building opens out onto the court by way of a stairway surmounted by a canopy with beautifully shaped columns and Ionic capitals which supports a dome roofed in scalloped tiles, providing access to a stairway with straight banisters and a landing, one of the first of its kind built in Toulouse (along with that of the Maison de Pierre).

The Cathédrale Saint-Étienne

From the outset, the cathedral disconcerts many people due to its strange form, the result of architectural modifications carried out since the Roman era. In the early Christian era, the Episcopal group established itself on the antique rampart near one of the gates. The buildings which occupied the site in the early Christian era remain unknown. We know that the Bishop Isarn found, upon his arrival at the Episcopal seat (1071) a church ruined and deserted by its clergy. In the general current of the Gregorian reforms, he improved the life of the canons who looked after the cathedral and undertook to rebuild the edifice. The vestiges can be seen on the walls of the current nave (particularly in a bulls-eye window where stones and bricks alternate, visible from the garden). The

Place Saint-Étienne, whose "griffoul" is the city's oldest public fountain (16th century). 17th and 18th century houses border this triangular square, which is completed by the façade of the Cathédrale Saint-Étienne.

Interior of the Cathédrale Saint-Étienne.

Keystone of the cathedral choir chapel sculpted by Kappellmeister de Rieux (14th century): Sainte-Catherine d'Alexandrie.

church was transformed at the beginning of the 13th century; the outer walls of the Romanesque edifice were used to support the vast nave as we now know it. The cathedral affirmed some of the developing principals of gothic architecture in the Midi: a vast space without side aisles, vaulted in a single span 19.5 meters wide between 1210 and 1230. The vaults, which were rounded, were supported by rectangular ribs, lateral arches and other supporting structures that were grounded on pilasters by the intermediary of the Romanesque capitals, which were thus put to new use.

To the West, the façade received a large rose window (most of whose elements were handed over to the Musée des Augustins following the most recent restoration). On the inside, the window overlooked a gallery covered with cowled arches. Only the three western bays of the building have been preserved. We know nothing of the placement of the chevet, which disappeared during the construction of the present choir. The choir was the result of the immense project envisioned by the Great prelate Bertrand de l'Isle-Jourdain; to level all previous buildings and undertake the construction of a completely new cathedral in a style close to that of the Cathédrale de Narbonne, which belonged to northern French architecture. Towards 1272,

the choir began to be built, and in huge proportions: twice as large as the nave, including five bays, surrounded by an ambulatory and radiating chapels. The death of the bishop, and the resulting loss of financing, the dismemberment of the diocese in 1317, and then the general crisis of the 14th century, all contributed to the halt in construction, which stopped at the level of the triforium and was covered with a "temporary" wooden roof. After several attempts to restart construction under Archbishop Bernard du Rosier, Jean d'Orléans (1503-1533) built a large pillar which marked the beginning of a transept, but which was never completed. In 1609, a fire destroyed the wooden roof and the church's furnishings. In order to avoid the repetition of such a disaster, the archbishop and the canons decided to vault the choir, and the architect who was entrusted with the work was Pierre Levesville. He raised the height of the windows and closed the vault at 28 meters above the ground instead of the 40 initially planned. The choir served the canons and the archbishop (the worshippers were placed in the nave, which was more or less well connected to the choir). Pierre Monge sculpted the choir stalls. It was only at the beginning of the 20th century that the link between the two parts was completed by the creation of the northern portal. The western portal had been splen-

Stalls in the cathedral, sculpted by Pierre Monge after the great fire which ravaged the choir during the night of December 9th, 1609.

didly rebuilt in the 15th century by the archbishop Pierre du Moulin. The steeple shows the same stratification; on a Romanesque portion which was extended in the Gothic era, Jean d'Orléans built the current steeple.

It is thus this surprising juxtaposition of amputated and incomplete edifices, which forms the cathedral today. But far from being isolated, it is the center of a very active neighborhood, which has seen its most precious landmarks disappear one after another. The district was formerly marked to the east by the Rempart de la Cité , to the north by the cathedral, to the west by the seat of the diocese (the building, reconstructed in the 18th century has been taken over by the Prefecture) and to the south by the canons' lodgings. A large cloister was attached to the southern end of the cathedral, and its arcature was formed of columns, which were alternately simple and gemelled; the angles of the galleries were formed of pillars decorated with marble relief sculptures. In the eastern gallery was the chapter house, which was the source of elegant and refined relief sculptures, representing the apostles, and created by Gilabertus and his workteam during the years 1135-1140 (now housed in the Musée des Augustins).

The cloister was delimited to the south by the Église Saint-Jacques whose origins, undoubtebly, go back to the early Christian era. This very large group of buildings disappeared in 1811 following the decision to extend the Rue Sainte-Anne – which had previously ended at the cloisters – to the Porte Saint-Étienne. The Chapelle Saint-Anne was built around 1830 in the place of the Église Saint-Jacques, in a neo-Roman style and along a north-south axis.

The Grand-Rond and the Promenades

From the Cathédrale Saint-Étienne, the Allées François-Verdier lead to the Grand-Rond. In the second half of the 18th century, Toulouse was receptive to new ideas regarding urban development, whose goal was to increase the well-being of the inhabitants while simultaneously improving the city's economic potential. It is in this perspective that we must regard projects such as the construction of the wharves, the Canal de Brienne, Place du Capitole and Place Saint-Cyprien, and of the Grand-Rond. In the latter case, the prime developer was Louis de Mondran. From the Grand-Rond, a vast oval garden with an ornamental pond, radiated six large avenues. In each of them, the

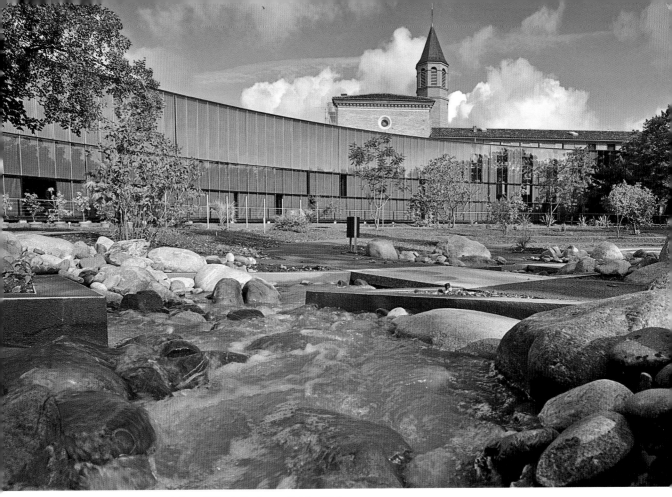

The Natural History Museum (photo Ville de Toulouse, Patrice Nin).

center divider was planted and two lanes were reserved for traffic. The project was carried out between 1752 and 1754, but the housing construction program, which was to have accompanied it was never put into effect.

The Église Saint-Exupère

The Discalced Carmelites had established their monastery outside the city walls, near the Porte Montgaillard. The first mass was celebrated in the monastery's unfinished church in 1623. Initially dedicated to Saint Joseph whose probable representation (unless it is that of Saint Christopher) placed above a fine classical portal, is a mould from the piece sculpted by Gervais Drouet.

The rib-vaulted nave, flanked by six chapels, has preserved its lavish stucco decoration which surrounds the windows and frames several antique paintings. In the choir, modified in the 19th century, ten paintings by Jean-Baptiste Despax (18th century), originating from the ceiling of the now-destroyed Église des Pénitents Noirs. This initial church became the parish of Saint-Exupère in 1807 and its classical cloister was preserved.

The Natural History Museum

Initially founded in 1796 by Philippe Picot de Lapeyrouse in the disused buildings of the former Discalced Carmelite convent, whose so-called "de Frescati Gardens" received botanical specimens from the town's Academy of Sciences and formed the basis of the Botanic Garden (Jardin des Plantes) we see today, Toulouse' Natural History Museum finally became established in its present location in 1865.

Second only to the one in Paris in its particular speciality, the museum has recently undergone complete renovation including a major extension into a new building designed by architect Jean-Paul Viguier. Its long curved glass façade provides a panoramic view of the botanic garden which was also redesigned and restructured. The new Museum opened its doors to the public again on 25th January 2008. The visit begins with a new view of Planet Earth and its position in Space, with its mineral wealth, movements and climates. Every aspect of life is then shown with its current classification, including Man. The history of living things is displayed from their earliest days, in the midst of geological and climatic transformations. Their basic characteristics (the need to feed, move, provide protection, reproduce,

FROM TOP TO BOTTOM

Detail from the Maison Lamotte, attributed to Urbain Vitry, Place de la Trinité (1830). The 19th century taste for ornament and classicism, is evidenced here by the Roman order of the façade and the two terracotta statues of Hermes and Pomona.

Façade of the Église des Saint-Exupère: detail of portal.

Thousands of children visit the Jardin des Plantes every year, so a certain number of the remains of buildings which risked being totally destroyed have been reconstructed: here a section of the old town rampart has been restored which served as the base of mediaeval house.

Musée Georges-Labit: narrative pediment of Preah Pithu, in sandstone, from the late 12th or early 13th centuries.

perceive and communicate) are highlighted and explained. Man's role in the ecosystem, which he often endangers by the cultural, social and technological dimensions of his actions, is finally placed centre stage to increase public awareness of the situation and improve our behaviour.

The Jardin des plantes
and the Monument de la Résistance

After the visit to the Jardin Botanique Henri-Gaussen (now open to the public from April to October, Tuesdays to Fridays), the stroller should cross the Jardin des Plantes, with its rare perfumes, where the remains of a mediaeval house, set upon a portion of the 1st century Roman wall, have been rebuilt, together with two gates (16th and 17th centuries) from the Capitole. The garden joins up with the end of the Allées Frédéric-Mistral where the impressive monument to the glory of the Résistance was buried. By continuing along the Allées des Demoiselles, the interesting departmental Musée de la Résistance et de la Déportation (N°52) is worth a visit, before arriving at the end of the alley, at the dry dock with its boat shed. By following the towpath along the Canal du Midi, the visitor will arrive at the entrance to the Musée Georges-Labit garden, with its three arcades.

The Cité de l'Espace, from outside.

The Musée Georges-Labit

Toulouse owes its surprising museum of Oriental art to Georges Labit (born in 1862 and who died prematurely in 1899), a son born to merchants from Toulouse. Attracted by distant voyages from a young age, he discovered Asia and brought back photographs and objects including engravings, weapons, porcelain and ivory from Japan. After his death, his father donated to the town the collections which he had assembled and the curious neo-Moorish style villa which he had built in Rue du Japon.

It is one of the rare museums in France where one can discover and appreciate works, often of the highest quality, from India, Gandhâra, Cambodia, Champâ, Annam, Siam, Laos, Java, Tibet, Nepal, China and Japan. The Musée Georges-Labit also exhibits the municipal collections of Coptic and Egyptian antiquities.

The Cité de l'Espace

Toulouse owes its economic expansion, during the 20th century, in part to the aeronautic industry. It all began in 1917 when an industrialist from the north of France, Georges-Latécoère moved his aeronautic construction plant to Toulouse. The great adventure of the conquest of the air, begun in time of war, ushered in a new era with legendary pilots such as Antoine de Saint Exupéry, Jean Mermoz, Didier Daurat, Henri Guillaumet and others. For several years now the Cité de l'Espace (to the east of Toulouse, Rue Jean Gonord) has exhibited among others the Russian space station Mir, several satellites, a planetarium for the discovery of the universe and simulator experiences. In addition, exhibitions, activities, and conferences all make a considerable contribution to the great success that this new center of Toulouse culture has been enjoying.

1. Manufacture des Tabacs (19th C).
2. Moulins and Usine du Bazacle.
3. Remains of the Great cloister of the Chartreux (17th C).
4. Former Séminaire Calvet (18th C).
5. Former Hôtel Dubarry.
6. Former Séminaire Saint-Charles (18th C).
7. Former Collège du Périgord (17th C) and Tour Maurand (12th C).
8. Chapelle des Carmélites (17th C).
9. Former shop « Au Capitole » (beginning of 20th C).
10. Église Sainte-Marie-des-Anges (19th C).
11. « La Dépêche » building (20th C).
12. Hôtel du Sénéchal.
13. Former Collège de l'Esquile (16th - 17th C).
14. Remains of the Couvent des Cordeliers (13th - 14th C).
15. Collège de Foix (15th C).
16. Former Couvent des Dames du Sac (17th C), Hôpital Larrey and then, Conservatoire.
17. Former Caserne de la Mission (17th C).
18. Hôtel de Bernuy.
19. Hôtel de Maleprade.
20. Café « Le Bibent ».
21. Hôtel Duranti.
22. Église Saint-Jérôme (17th C).
23. Former Commanderie Saint-Antoine du T. (17th C).
24. Hôtel de La Fage.
25. Hôtel de Guillaume Bernuy.
26. Hôtel de Sapte.
27. Tour de Pierre Séguy (15th C) and Hôtel du capitoul Jean Bolé.
28. Hôtel Dumay and Musée du Vieux-Toulouse.
29. Hôtel Comère.
30. Former cloister of the Couvent des Ursulines and former Poste.
30 bis. Tour de Jean de Gayssion.
31. Hôtel Lagorrée.
32. Tour des Ysalguier (15th C), former Hôtel d'Espagne.
33. Hôtel d'Olmières.
34. Hôtel de Nupces.
35. Hôtel de Pierre Delfau.
36. Hôtel d'Assézat and Fondation Bemberg.
37. Hôtel du capitoul Ricardy.
38. Tour Vinhas (13th C).
39. Logis de Boysson and Hôtel de Cheverry.
40. Maison d'Arnaud de Brucelles.
41. Maison du capitoul Jean de Boscredon.
42. Hôtel Delpech (tower 16th C).
43. Hôtel d'Astorg and Saint-Germain.
44. Hôtel Desplats.
45. Tour de Serta (16th C).
46. Hôtel Dassier.
47. Hôtel de Tornié de Vaillac.
48. Maison (19th C).
49. Former Collège Saint-Martial (14th - 16th C).
50. Hôtel Dupin.
51. Maison Calas.
52. Maison (17th C).
53. Hôtel de Pierre Bruni.
54. Hôtel de la Mamye.
55. Hôtel d'Aldéguier.
56. Hôtel de Pierre.
57. Hôtel Saint-Jean.
58. Hôtel Molinier or de Felzins.
59. Hôtel du baron de Montbel.
60. Hôtel de Villepigne.
61. Hôtel Le Mazuyer.

62. Hôtel de Chalvet and then, de Pins.
63. Maison de saint Dominique and former Couvent des Réparatrices.
64. Hôtel du capitoul Jérôme Taverne and Tour de Noël Rolle.
65. Hôtel de Guillaume de Lespinasse.
66. Hôtel du capitoul Jean Marvejol.
67. Hôtel d'Olivier Pastoureau (tower 16th C).
68. Hôtel Reversac de Celès de Marsac.
69. Hôtel Boissy.
70. Chapel and cloister of the Prieuré Saint-Antoine-du-Salin.
71. Temple, former Trésorerie royale.
72. Capitoul Pierre de Ruppe tower.
73. Hôtel de Paucy (« Maison de la Belle Paule »).
74. Hôtel Fajole.
75. Église du Jésus (19th C).
76. Chapelle de Nazareth (16th C).
77. Hôtel Davisard.
78. Hôtel de Potier-Laterrasse (overlooking Renaissance courtyard).
79. Tour de Guillaume Carreri.
80. Hôtel Labat de Mourlens.
81. Hôtel du Vieux-Raisin.
82. Hôtel de Pins gallery.
83. Hôtel de Ciron.
83 bis. Maison de Pons Imbert.
84. Hôtel de Castellane.
85. « Maison romane »
86. Hôtel and Tour de Bonnefoy.
87. Hôtel de Ramondy.
88. Hôtel de Candie de Saint-Simon.
89. Hôtel de Puivert.
90. Hôtel de Campistron.
91. Hôtel d'Orbessan.
92. Tour de Raynier and Hôtel de Virvin.
93. Hôtel d'Espie.
94. Hôtel d'Ayguevives.
95. Hôtel du capitoul Pierre Dahus and Tour des Tournoër.
96. Hôtel Mansencal.
97. Hôtel de Pennautier.
98. Hôtel de Tappie de Vinsac.
99. Hôtel (16th C).
99 bis. Hôtel de Sacère-Murat.
100. Hôtel de Castelpers.
101. Hôtel de Sevin-Mansencal.
102. Hôtel de Panat.
103. Hôtel de Bonfontan.
104. Hôtel de Froidour.
105. Hôtel du capitoul Jean Catel.
106. Hôtel du conseiller de Maran.
107. Hôtel de Cambon.
108. Hôtel du Bourg.
109. Former Archives du diocèse building (18th C).
110. Hôtel Lestang (17th C).
111. Maison (17th C).
112. Hôtel du comte de Paulo.
113. Hôtel d'Ulmo.
114. Hôtel de Castagné d'Auriac.
115. Palais Niel.
116. Hôtel Thomas (remains of the Hôtel de Pins).
117. Hôtel Dupuy-Montaut.
118. Monastère des Feuillants.
119. Musée des compagnons.
120. Musée d'histoire de la médecine
121. Abattoirs, Centre d'art moderne et contemporain.

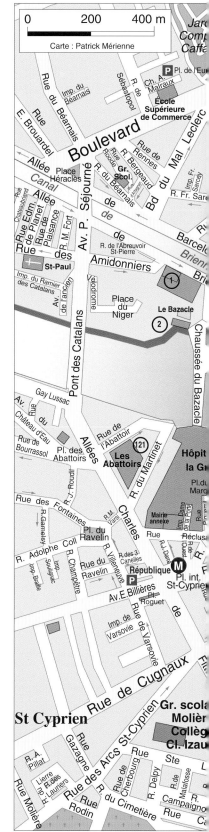

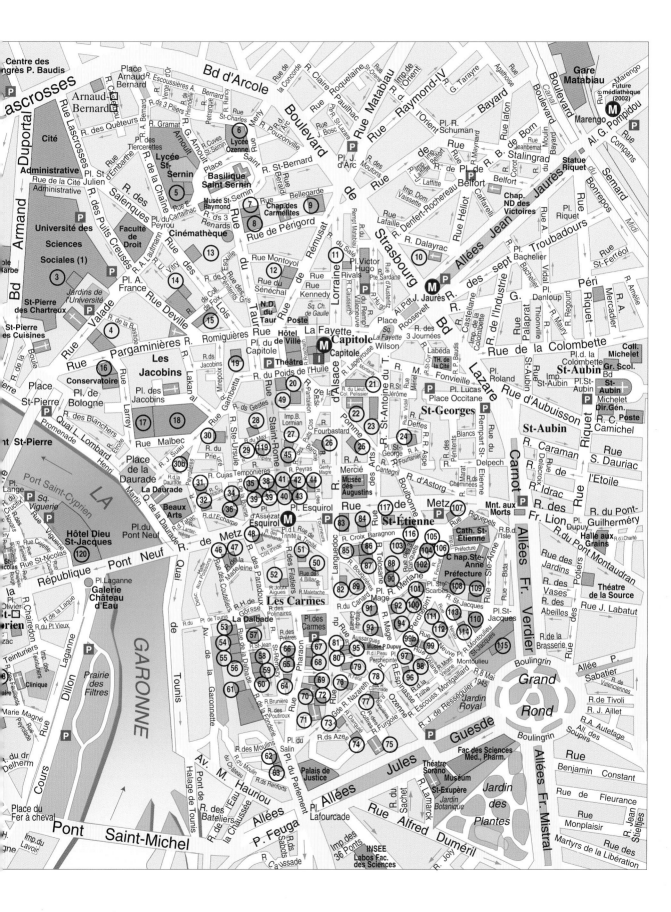

The canal de Brienne was dug in the 18th century to link the Garonne upstream from Bazacle with the Midi-Canal. The two canals met at the Bassin de l'Embouchure and the meeting point is marked by the Ponts-Jumeaux, decorated with a large relief sculpture created by François Lucas (1775).

List of contents

© Éditions Sud Ouest, 2002. Ce livre a été imprimé par Pollina à Luçon (85) – France. Graphiste presse papier
ISBN : 978-2-87901-474-6 – Editeur : 1226.02.03.06.08 – N° d'impression : L46885